THE
POWER
OF
PURPLE

women of purpose
in scripture

John W. Stanko

urbanpress

The Power of Purple
by John W. Stanko
Copyright © 2018 John W. Stanko

ISBN # 978-1-63360-092-8

For Worldwide Distribution   Printed in the U.S.A.

Urban Press
P.O. Box 8881
Pittsburgh, PA 15221-0881 USA
412.646.2780
www.urbanpress.us

Introduction

God began to reveal my purpose message to me in 1981 after I survived a failed business venture. I had opportunities to teach about purpose over the next few years, but it wasn't until 1989 that I had the chance to teach it more fully and that was in, of all places, a Florida penitentiary. Then in 1991, I made my first public purpose presentation in Pismo Beach, California and the rest is history.

When I first understood and taught purpose, I had this God-inspired thought: "Men will invite you to speak on purpose, but women will hear you." That statement has proved to be true. I am not implying that men have not heard and applied the purpose message, but many more women have identified and pursued the implications of the message, and it has borne much fruit. I would jokingly say in my early presentations, "Eve's purpose was not to launder Adam's underwear because Adam didn't have any underwear." I think it got the point across.

Men wrote the Bible in a world that was male-dominated, and much has been made of that fact. Yet, there is quite a bit of material about how God used women, and we don't have to squeeze or contort the Scriptures to find those examples. Therefore, I thought it would be good to highlight those stories and examples first in my weekly online publication, *The Monday Memo*, and now in this book. Let me say that while the stories are about women, they are also purpose stories that apply to all people, women and men.

In the pages that follow, I will present 19 case studies or profiles of women who distinguished themselves in the Bible by expressing their purpose (Esther has two chapters, Mary the mother of Jesus has two, Hannah has three, and two women are combined into one profile, in case you wonder how I did the math). In each profile, we will look at their story and extract purpose concepts and principles that are relevant to your life. We will go to war with Deborah, laugh with Sarah, travel with Mary Magdalene, and go to a prayer meeting with Lydia, the purveyor of purple cloth. I used Lydia's business as the title for this book, for she found purpose power in the color purple, which is a favorite color of many women I know.

I present *The Purple of Power* to continue the trend that started when I introduced my purpose message. Women have been touched, challenged, and liberated by the message and I trust that you will experience the same result in the pages of this book. Thank you for reading, and may the purpose power of your purple, whatever expression of life that represents, be even more pronounced and fruitful because you have read these inspiring profiles.

John W. Stanko
Pittsburgh, PA
June 2018

ESTHER
Queen for More Than a Day

When I was growing up, there was a popular TV show that started with the announcer asking, "Would *you* like to be queen for a day?" The show would then interview four women, asking them questions about their lives and families. The last question would ask them what they needed to make their life easier, and then the audience would indicate which woman should be queen by their applause, measured by an "applause meter" to identify the winner who was then crowned queen for the day.

Your Place

Esther went through a similar process to become queen, but when she was selected from among all the women in the king's domain, she was appointed queen for life. Once she was queen, we learn that Esther was instrumental in saving her fellow Jews from destruction by being in the right place at the right time. How did she get to this place where she fulfilled her purpose, being used by God in a special way? Let's look at three points that will answer that question:

1. Your past doesn't prevent you from fulfilling your purpose, unless you allow it to do so.

"Mordecai had a cousin named Hadassah, whom he had brought up because she had neither father nor mother" (Esther 2:7a). Esther was an orphan. What's more, she wasn't even raised by an aunt or grandparent. She was raised by her male cousin, Mordecai, in a foreign country where they were both minorities. Thus, Esther didn't have much going for her in the natural. She had God with her, however, and someone once said, "You plus God are a majority no matter how many others there are." Do you believe that? If you do, then when will start acting like it?

2. You may be taking your obvious purpose for granted.

"This girl, who was also known as Esther, was lovely in form and features, and Mordecai had taken her as his own daughter when her father and mother died" (Esther 2:7b). I love the way the Bible describes Esther. One version states that she was beautiful "in face and form." In other words, Esther was a beauty queen! That may not seem significant or even a bit "worldly," but her beauty was an important part of her purpose. You can become so accustomed to who you are that you miss the obvious, which is why you may not be able to describe your purpose. Your purpose may be so natural or "unspectacular" to you that it is hard to recognize. You may even take your beauty or some other feature for granted, when it may hold a key to fulfilling your purpose.

3. God wants to build on your strengths and not your weaknesses.

"When the king's order and edict had been

proclaimed, many girls were brought to the citadel of Susa and put under the care of Hegai. Esther also was taken to the king's palace and entrusted to Hegai, who had charge of the harem. The girl pleased him and won his favor. Immediately he provided her with her beauty treatments and special food. He assigned to her seven maids selected from the king's palace and moved her and her maids into the best place in the harem" (Esther 2:8-9).

Esther was beautiful, so what did God do? He surrounded her with people who would make her more beautiful. Too often, we spend time fretting about our weaknesses and consequently spend even more time trying to be who we are not. If you're doing that, please stop. Focus on your strengths and be the best expression of who God made you to be. God isn't interested in well-rounded individuals. He wants to use specialists who have focused on being the best they can be. That's the power of purpose.

Who Are You?

So who are you? Are you beautiful? Can you play the piano? Speak before audiences? Play or coach basketball? Can you write poetry? Whatever it is, ask yourself how you can be even better in those areas where you are already strong. Take time to focus on your strengths and please don't allow your painful past, even your failures, to determine the extent to which God can use you today. God used Esther's beauty to open doors for her and He will use your strengths to do the same for you, if you don't try to diminish or ignore them. Make up your mind to follow in Esther's footsteps and be the best you can be.

ESTHER
Right Place, Right Time

In the first chapter, we started a purpose profile on Esther. Esther was an orphan who was looked after by her cousin, Mordecai. She was beautiful and was selected to be queen when the previous queen displeased the king. God used her beauty to strategically position her where she could save her people in their day of trouble. For her role, the Spirit named an Old Testament book after her that included her story and that of her cousin-caretaker. What additional purpose lessons can you learn from Esther's promotion that will help you in your own life of purpose? Let's answer that question now.

Purpose comes looking for you.

Esther didn't have to look for her purpose; her purpose came looking for her:

Then the king's personal attendants proposed,
"Let a search be made for beautiful young virgins
for the king. Let the king appoint commissioners
in every province of his realm to bring all these
beautiful girls into the harem at the citadel

of Susa. Let them be placed under the care of Hegai, the king's eunuch, who is in charge of the women; and let beauty treatments be given to them. Then let the girl who pleases the king be queen instead of Vashti." This advice appealed to the king, and he followed it (Esther 2:2-4).

They discovered Esther and chose her to be among those women under consideration, and they eventually selected her to be the new queen. As you examine your purpose, ask yourself: What always finds me that needs done? What group or kinds of people seek me out for counsel, encouragement, or help?

If you can answer those questions, you will have important clues to help you clarify your purpose. One thing that regularly happens to me, for instance, no matter where I am in the world, is that people ask me for directions—an expression of my purpose to create order out of chaos. I never have to go looking for chaos; chaos always comes looking for me.

The Right Place at the Right Time

After Esther was chosen to be the new queen, a crisis arose among her fellow Jews. The king had an aide named Haman, who hated the Jews with a passion. He convinced the king (who was unaware that Esther was a Jew) to issue an edict that all the Jews were to be exterminated throughout the kingdom. What was Esther to do? Her cousin Mordecai gave her good advice, as usual:

When Esther's words were reported to Mordecai, he sent back this answer: "Do not think that because you are in the king's house you alone of all the Jews will escape. For if you remain silent at this time, relief and deliverance for the Jews will arise from another place, but you and your father's family will perish. *And who knows but that you have come to royal position for such a time as this?"* (Esther 4:12-14, emphasis added).

The second point is that purpose puts you in the right place at the right time.

When you function in your purpose, there is a sense that God is helping you accomplish what you are doing without you having to exert energy or time to make something happen. When someone needs directions, I happen to come along and for whatever reason, they choose me out of the crowd to ask where to go. I could not plan that if I wanted to. It is a small way in which I know that God uses me to help others and it flows naturally. It is part of my purpose to create order out of chaos.

Ask yourself these questions: When am I most in "the flow?" When do I most seem to be in the right place at the right time? What need or needs do I always seem to be properly positioned to meet? Answers to those questions will most certainly help you clarify your purpose and then express it as Esther did on the throne she obtained through her God-given beauty and not her own efforts.

LYDIA
Purple Power

In Roman times, purple was the color of the elite. Emperors and senators wore purple tunics and togas and since there were no synthetic dyes, natural coloring needed to be found to produce such regal robes. There was a tiny shellfish in the area of Macedonia that produced one drop of precious purple coloring in its little body, and there was industry built around harvesting, extracting, and then applying the purple liquid to cloth. It is reported that the purple cloth was literally worth its weight in silver! Knowing that bit of history, let's look at our next woman of purpose, a woman named Lydia mentioned in Acts 16.

Paul Meets Purple

Luke introduced Lydia with the following account in Acts:

> From Troas we put out to sea and sailed straight for Samothrace, and the next day we went on to Neapolis. From there we traveled to Philippi, a Roman colony and the leading city of that district of Macedonia. And we stayed there several

days. On the Sabbath we went outside the city gate to the river, where we expected to find a place of prayer. We sat down and began to speak to the women who had gathered there. One of those listening was a woman from the city of Thyatira named Lydia, a dealer in purple cloth. She was a worshiper of God. The Lord opened her heart to respond to Paul's message. When she and the members of her household were baptized, she invited us to her home. "If you consider me a believer in the Lord," she said, "come and stay at my house." And she persuaded us (Acts 16:11-15).

This "chance" meeting between Lydia and Paul was another encounter between Roman power and the message of the gospel. Here was a woman who had built a significant business that serviced only the richest, most powerful people in the Roman Empire. When she heard Paul's gospel message, she submitted to the call of God to fellowship with Him through Christ. Lydia was probably not married when she met Paul. After her conversion, Lydia, who was already a worshiper of God, was free to direct all her considerable wealth and resources to minister to the needs of Paul's team and also plant a church that met in her home, which had servants and space to meet (indicating she was a woman of means): "After Paul and Silas came out of the prison, they went to Lydia's house, where they met with the brothers and sisters and encouraged them" (Acts 16:40).

Purpose Lessons

What can we learn from this woman's life who harnessed the power of purple to build a successful business?

1. She did not need to be married to have purpose.

2. Lydia found room for spirituality while traveling and running a successful business

3. Lydia had money, servants, and property at her disposal, and she used them to fund the spread of the gospel in her area and beyond.

How do I know that she carried out what I wrote in point three? I don't; it is only an educated guess based on what Paul wrote in Philippians 4:14-18:

> Yet it was good of you to share in my troubles. Moreover, as you Philippians know, in the early days of your acquaintance with the gospel, when I set out from Macedonia, not one church shared with me in the matter of giving and receiving, except you only; for even when I was in Thessalonica, you sent me aid more than once when I was in need. Not that I desire your gifts; what I desire is that more be credited to your account. I have received full payment and have more than enough. I am amply supplied, now that I have received from Epaphroditus the gifts you sent. They are a fragrant offering, an acceptable sacrifice, pleasing to God.

It makes sense that the church meeting in Lydia's home would send Paul financial help and that Lydia would spearhead the effort to support her favorite apostle. This woman of purpose supported the apostle of purpose to reach out to others to find and fulfill their purpose in Christ, including women in areas outside Macedonia. In a sense, Lydia was supporting missions outreaches through her business acumen, taking the profits of sales to the

Roman aristocracy to fund the ministry of the Word.

If you are a woman, I encourage you to unleash the full power of your vision for cosmetics, fashion, modeling, hair-care, or any other business endeavor in your heart to build your own business. I also urge you to use the proceeds from your endeavor not only to provide for your household, but also for those who have impacted and directed your spiritual life. We need some Elizabeth Ardens, Estee Lauders, Christie Brinkleys, and Oprah Winfreys who aren't afraid of the power of their own "purple" ideas that will then be used to help extend God's kingdom. That won't happen until you take seriously the power of your own purple ideas and act in faith to see them become a part of the world around you.

DEBORAH
A Blow to the Head

In this next profile, let's look at the Old Testament prophet, Deborah. We never hear much about Deborah perhaps because her story is short and contained within a book to which we don't often pay attention – the book of Judges. Then again, perhaps we don't hear more about her because she violated all the norms of Old Testament life. She was a woman who made her "name" not because of who she was married to, but because of her spiritual gift and wisdom:

> Now Deborah, a prophet, the wife of Lappidoth, was leading Israel at that time. She held court under the Palm of Deborah between Ramah and Bethel in the hill country of Ephraim, and the Israelites went up to her to have their disputes decided (Judges 4:4-5).

A Woman Was Leading Israel

Deborah was leading Israel! Let that statement sink into your mind—a woman was leading the people of God. She was not doing so because she was queen or had inherited the role from her husband who had the role but had died. Her leadership emerged from the experience that the people had with her, for they recognized God was with her when she judged and spoke.

Israel was oppressed in Deborah's day by the Canaanites who were led by a man named Sisera. Deborah summoned the head of the Naphtali tribe, named Barak, and told him to assemble an army and march against Sisera's superior forces. If he did, Deborah promised that God would grant him the victory. When Barak hesitated and insisted that Deborah go with him, Deborah agreed, but said,

> "Certainly I will go with you," said Deborah. "But because of the course you are taking, the honor will not be yours, for the Lord will deliver Sisera into the hands of a woman." So Deborah went with Barak to Kedesh (Judges 4:9).

Just as Deborah had prophesied, Barak routed the enemies of Israel: "Sisera, meanwhile, fled on foot to the tent of Jael, the wife of Heber the Kenite, because there was an alliance between Jabin king of Hazor and the family of Heber the Kenite" (Judges 4:17). It was then that Deborah's other prediction came true: Sisera was not slain by his rival warriors but by the woman to whom he had fled for protection:

> But Jael, Heber's wife, picked up a tent peg and a hammer and went quietly to him while he lay fast asleep, exhausted. She drove the peg through his temple into the ground, and he died. Just then Barak came by in pursuit of Sisera, and Jael went out to meet him. "Come," she said, "I will show you the man you're looking for." So

he went in with her, and there lay Sisera with the tent peg through his temple—dead (Judges 4:21-22).

A Blow to the Head

When Deborah assumed her God-given role, the Bible does not report it was because no man wanted the job. Deborah led because God chose her, knowing full well she was a female. What's more, when Deborah accepted her call, it made room for another woman to stand up and lead, and her name was Jael, who dealt with Sisera with one fatal blow to his head.

This lesson in this story is similar to what William Booth, founder of the Salvation Army, once said when asked why he sent so many women into the slums of London to reach out to the lost: "Some of my best men are women!" This was certainly true in the case of Deborah and Jael, and it may be true for you too.

If you are a woman, have you been stifling your own gift, trapped and restricted by your own erroneous philosophy that only men can lead in certain situations? If someone has a gift to lead or speak or write, who gave them that gift? Was God aware of their gender when He bestowed that gift? If God is not offended to give that gift and then see it used, then why should you, or anyone else for that matter, be offended when they express that gift? Why would God give a woman a gift, then not permit her to deploy it? That makes no sense.

The judges of Israel rose to leadership based on their gift and purpose, not based on their gender or family connections. God knows your sex when He calls you, whether male or female, and if He is comfortable with who you are to fulfill an assigned role, then you should be as well. There are some strongholds that are waiting for you to pick up a spiritual hammer and peg and deal the enemy of God's people a fatal blow to the head. If you happen to be a woman, you only need God's permission to do so. I suggest you get on with the work that God has given you to do, and follow in Deborah's—and Jael's—footsteps to play your part in setting God's people free.

WOMEN AUTHORS IN THE BIBLE

I'm sure I have your undivided attention based on the title of this chapter. It has been taught that the Bible was written by men, but I want to dispute that widely-held belief. While men may have written the Bible, not all the words originated from their minds or mouths, and I am not talking about dialogue that included quotes from a woman's mouth. Let me explain what I mean.

The Inspired Word

The Bible is the inspired word of God, isn't it? We maintain that the Holy Spirit moved on the hearts of the writers to write what the Spirit wanted written. Evangelicals believe that the very words used were inspired by God. Therefore, if a man was recording what the Spirit inspired a woman to say, then that woman was the source of the inspiration, and the writer was also inspired, but only to record for posterity what that woman had to say.

Having said that, consider the women who contributed inspired words to the inspired Word. Consider Mary's words that Luke recorded after her encounter with her cousin:

And Mary said: "My soul glorifies the Lord and my spirit rejoices in God my Savior, for he has been mindful of the humble state of his servant. From now on all generations will call me bless-ed, for the Mighty One has done great things for me—holy is his name" (Luke 1:46-49).

Who really "wrote" that prayer? Did Luke write it or did Mary compose it and Luke reported it? The correct answer is the latter: Mary "wrote" it, Luke passed it on. Then let's consider Hannah's prayer in 2 Samuel:

Then Hannah prayed and said: "My heart re-joices in the Lord; in the Lord my horn is lifted high. My mouth boasts over my enemies, for I delight in your deliverance. There is no one holy like the Lord; there is no one besides you; there is no Rock like our God" (1 Samuel 2:1-2).

Isn't that the same as Mary's words? A woman ut-tered them and the man, recognizing that the Spirit in-spired the woman's words, wrote them down for others to read and benefit from.

Then There was Deborah

Then there was Deborah, whose leadership we looked at in the last profile. After Deborah urged King Barak to pursue and defeat God's enemies, we read this account:

On that day, Deborah and Barak son of Abinoam sang this song:

"When the princes in Israel take the lead, when the people willingly offer themselves—praise the Lord! Hear this, you kings! Listen, you rulers! I, even I, will sing to the Lord; I will praise the Lord, the God of Israel, in song.

"When you, Lord, went out from Seir, when you marched from the land of Edom, the earth shook, the heavens poured, the clouds poured down water. The mountains quaked before the Lord, the One of Sinai, before the Lord, the God of Israel.

"In the days of Shamgar son of Anath, in the days of Jael, the highways were abandoned; travelers took to winding paths. Villagers in Israel would not fight; they held back until I, Deborah, arose, until I arose, a mother in Israel. God chose new leaders when war came to the city gates, but not a shield or spear was seen among forty thousand in Israel. My heart is with Israel's princes, with the willing volunteers among the people. Praise the Lord!" (Judges 5:1-9).

Even if Deborah's role was to co-author this song, she still contributed to the collection of God's inspired words that today we know as the Bible. If God used Mary, Hannah, and Deborah, then it is safe to assume that there were other women He inspired to do His work that the Bible does not record. Nothing has changed today, for He still wants to use the female half of His human creation to do His bidding. The question is: Will that female half step up and take their role, or shrink back because of bad theology that God doesn't "use" women, or only uses them to populate the earth?

How about it, sister? Are you ready to step up and be used of God and fulfill your purpose? How about it, brother? Are you ready to sing a duet with a sister in the Lord like Barak did with Deborah? The world needs *all*

God's children, men and women, to play their part in this wonderful realm called God's kingdom. I hope you won't play small or not at all, but will perform to the full extent of God's purpose for you.

MARY
She was There

We have looked at Lydia and Deborah. Now let's go back to the New Testament to look at Mary, the mother of Jesus, and start out by saying that her purpose was *not* to give birth to Jesus. In fact, no woman's purpose is to give birth to any child. That statement may surprise you, so before you write off what I wrote, you had better read on.

More than a Mother

I maintain that childbirth is not a life purpose, but a role that some women fulfill for quite a few years. They give birth, nurture, and care for their children, but eventually those children are going to move on. Problems can arise when the child wants to go but the mother derives so much of her identify and fulfillment from the child that she cannot let him or her go. I have always taught that a woman has purpose *before* she marries and *after* her children are gone and her husband precedes her to glory. Of course, there are many women who do not have children, so does that mean they are purposeless or less than those women who are mothers? Absolutely not! Therefore, if Mary's purpose was not to give birth to Jesus, what was it?

We find Mary's purpose statement uttered by Elizabeth in Luke 1:45: "Blessed is she who has believed that the Lord would fulfill his promises to her!" Mary's purpose was to preserve, oversee, and participate by faith in the promises that were uttered where Jesus was concerned. To fulfill that purpose, Mary had to be present at all the important occasions in Jesus' life and ministry, and exercise faith that God would do through Jesus what He promised He would do. Consider these situations where Mary was present:

1. ". . . and all who heard it were amazed at what the shepherds said to them. But Mary treasured up all these things and pondered them in her heart" (Luke 2:18b-19). Mary was listening carefully to what was said about Jesus and kept those things in her heart, perhaps to share with Jesus, and certainly to share with the gospel writers.

2. "Then Simeon blessed them and said to Mary, his mother: 'This child is destined to cause the falling and rising of many in Israel, and to be a sign that will be spoken against, so that the thoughts of many hearts will be revealed. And a sword will pierce your own soul too'" (Luke 2:34-35). Mary's proximity to the events in Jesus' life would cause her much pain and some confusion.

3. "His mother said to the servants, 'Do whatever he tells you'" (John 2:5). Mary instigated the start of Jesus' public ministry at the wedding feast in Cana.

4. "When his family heard about this, they went to take charge of him, for they said, 'He is out of his mind'" (Mark 3:21). Like John the Baptist, Mary was not clear on how Jesus would do what she had heard God promise, and in Mark 3 came to take Him home because she thought He was going off course.

5. "Near the cross of Jesus stood his mother, his mother's sister, Mary the wife of Clopas, and Mary Magdalene" (John 19:25). Mary finally got it straight and was there to watch her son die on the cross as a witness to God's plan.

6. "When Jesus saw his mother there, and the disciple whom he loved standing nearby, he said to her, "Woman, here is your son" (John 19:26). When Mary "sided" with Jesus, the rest of her children wanted nothing to do with her, so Jesus assigned His disciple John to care for His mother.

7. "They all joined together constantly in prayer, along with the women and Mary the mother of Jesus, and with his brothers" (Acts 1:14). After the resurrection, some of Jesus' family "saw the light" and were present in the upper room when the Spirit was poured out. In a sense, it was Jesus sending His mother a message saying, "I arrived and the trip was good. I'm home." Is it then safe to assume that Mary spoke in tongues as the others did on the day of Pentecost?

She Was There

In a sense, Mary's purpose was to be there to support, protect, and clarify the plan of God for the world through Jesus. She had great faith, was present from start to finish, and had a role in the explanation of what had taken place before and during Jesus' infancy. There is no way Matthew or Luke could have written their accounts of the Nativity without Mary's testimony.

Mary played an important purpose role that God had chosen for her. While it involved her son, Jesus, it was not simply to give birth and raise Him to be a good Jewish boy. Mary played a role in the plan of salvation, and is a good example of purpose. Throughout history, theologians have argued over Mary and who she was or was not. My view is that she was a woman of purpose whom God handpicked to help guide her son and His Son through to His appointed and chosen purpose. That makes Mary as important as any man in God's plan of salvation for the world.

HANNAH
Purpose Hair

In this chapter, let's look at Hannah's story in the opening chapters of 1 Samuel. In Old Testament times, a woman was under cultural pressure to bear children. We see the agony of women like Sarah, Rebekah, and Elizabeth encountered when they realized they were barren. That makes God's intervention on their behalf all the more special and moving when He removed their childless stigma. That being said, let's look at how this scenario of childlessness played out in Hannah's life.

Childless

Hannah was one of Elkanah's two wives, and we are told that Elkanah loved her more than his other wife named Penninah, which was small consolation for Hannah who was childless. The stigma of not having children was so overwhelming that Hannah was almost inconsolable over her condition, and her rival wife used her child-bearing ability to irritate Hannah, trying to win Elkanah's favor. This situation drove Hannah to her knees as she sought the Lord for relief from the burden she had to bear. As she sought the Lord, she made an interesting vow:

"Lord Almighty, if you will only look on your servant's misery and remember me, and not forget your servant but give her a son, then I will give him to the Lord for all the days of his life, and no razor will ever be used on his head" (1 Samuel 1:11).

Even though she was childless, she was surrendering to the Lord *what she did not have.* She abandoned her motherly instinct to help shape her child's life ("no razor will ever be used on his head"), refusing to use her hands or motherly instincts to mold what would come forth from the child in the way of gifts, calling, and purpose. It is a magnificent faith gesture that Hannah gave to God what she did not have, but what she was believing Him to give her.

Like Hannah, you may be waiting for your purpose, and you see others around you who are finding and flowing in theirs. Perhaps God is asking you to yield your purpose to Him, to abandon any tendency to shape it according to what you think looks best, *before* you know what it is. I did that as I waited for many long years to be released into my purpose. I vowed that I would go wherever God wanted me to go and say what He wanted me to say, and that vow led me to fifty nations carrying the purpose message as I went. My purpose hair grew in a way that God desired, and I have not tried to comb, color, or fashion it—I have simply let it grow in the way that God wanted it to grow.

Give it to the Lord

I did not choose my work in Africa or around the world; it chose me. God had something special in mind for Hannah, just like He did for me, but it required both of us to seek Him and surrender to His will. It involved tearful expressions of anguish and pain that were all part of God's plan. God gave Hannah a son, and He gave me a purpose. Both the son and my purpose grew to be something neither one of us could have imagined beforehand. Perhaps the same will be true for you. If so, it all starts with giving to God what He hasn't yet given to you, and promising not to comb your purpose hair whenever it starts to grow. We will return to Hannah's story in the next chapter, but for now, you have a job to do and that is to give to God what He hasn't yet bestowed upon you.

HANNAH
Giving It to the Lord

In the last chapter, we looked at Hannah's story when she gave to the Lord what she didn't have, but believed in faith that she had already received. Let's return to Hannah's story to see what else we can learn, man or woman, from this woman of faith and purpose.

Misunderstood

In the last chapter, we learned that God required Hannah to give her child to Him before she had any children to give. That indicates her conviction that she would conceive because she surrendered her son to God *before* she ever laid eyes on him in the natural, promising she would not comb his hair. She vowed not to shape and fashion what God was doing in her child's life to her own satisfaction or preference.

All that sounds super spiritual, which it was, but as soon as Hannah made this commitment, she was tested in two ways that involved the same man, Eli the chief priest. First, as Hannah prayed, she moved her lips but did not make a sound; her prayers were silent groans concerning her unfulfilled purpose:

As she kept on praying to the Lord, Eli observed her mouth. Hannah was praying in her heart, and her lips were moving but her voice was not heard. Eli thought she was drunk and said to her, "How long are you going to stay drunk? Put away your wine" (1 Samuel 1:12-14).

As if Hannah was not already in enough pain, she had to endure the biting and sarcastic criticism from the man of God. Eli did not properly discern what Hannah was going through, and did not bother to make inquiries. He simply jumped to the conclusion that Hannah was drunk, and curtly chastised her.

After Hannah explained, Eli did not apologize or investigate the cause for Hannah's agony so that he could stand with her in prayer. Probably embarrassed, he sought to dismiss her as quickly as possible: "Go in peace, and may the God of Israel grant you what you have asked of him" (1 Samuel 1:17).

Giving It to the Lord—Really

God heard Hannah's prayer (not Eli's) and she conceived and brought forth a son whom she named Samuel. Hannah had made a vow in her distress, and once the pain was gone, she was not going to back away from the vow. As soon as the child was weaned, she took him back to the house of the Lord to be raised there by the very man who had misjudged her spiritual condition. This man was not worthy of Hannah's sacrifice, but Hannah had given her situation to the Lord, and she was not going to renege on her vow:

After he was weaned, she took the boy with her, young as he was, along with a three-year-old bull, an ephah of flour and a skin of wine, and brought him to the house of the Lord at Shiloh. When the bull had been sacrificed, they brought the boy to Eli, and she said to him, "Pardon me, my lord. As surely as you live, I am the woman who stood here beside you praying to the Lord. I prayed for this child, and the Lord has granted me what I asked of him. So now I give him to the Lord. For his whole life he will be given over to the Lord." And he worshiped the Lord there (1 Samuel 1:24-28).

The lessons for us are clear from this story. Your purpose belongs to God; you cannot grab hold of it to use as you see fit. When you give your purpose future to the Lord, He will manage it as *He* sees fit, perhaps investing or injecting you into situations that are not to your liking or that do not fully appreciate the sacrifice you are making.

Finally, when you make a commitment to the Lord to do something, especially a vow you made in your pain, you need to follow through on your commitment when the pain is gone and God has answered your prayer. In the next chapter, we will look at one more lesson from Hannah's purposeful life. I hope you will do business with God and follow through on the vows you made in times of pain or suffering.

HANNAH
You Can't Out-Give God

In the last two chapters, we looked at the life of Hannah. We saw how she gave her first child to the Lord *before* she ever gave birth and then followed through on her commitment by yielding the child to serve with Eli, the priest who had misjudged and then ignored her as she poured her heart out to the Lord.

It may strike someone, maybe even you, that the entire process Hannah went through was a bit "unfair." Hannah agonized over her childless state while her rival wife, Peninnah, had multiple births and then somehow antagonized Hannah by "rubbing it in."

After much pain and suffering, Hannah finally gave birth, but then carried her young son off to be raised in a monastery of sorts, only to see him every now and then for the rest of her life, making a new garment for him every year. All godly parents dedicate their children to the Lord's service, but usually that child stays with them until they are of the age to go off for education or training. In Hannah's case, Samuel went off as a toddler and, in a sense, Hannah was once again childless.

The Rest of the Story

If the story had ended there, it would seem a bit unfair, but God is a just God, and it is impossible to out-give Him. First, God revived Hannah's reputation in the house of God. Whereas before Eli had ignored her, he eventually blessed her every time he saw her:

> But Samuel was ministering before the Lord—a boy wearing a linen ephod. Each year his mother made him a little robe and took it to him when she went up with her husband to offer the annual sacrifice. Eli would bless Elkanah and his wife, saying, "May the Lord give you children by this woman to take the place of the one she prayed for and gave to the Lord." Then they would go home (1 Samuel 2:18-20).

Then Hannah's personal worship life took on a whole new meaning as we see when we read her song to the Lord in 1 Samuel 2:1-10. Here is part of that song:

> "My heart rejoices in the Lord; in the Lord my horn is lifted high. My mouth boasts over my enemies, for I delight in your deliverance. There is no one holy like the Lord; there is no one besides you; there is no Rock like our God" (1 Samuel 2:1-2).

It doesn't seem like Hannah resented giving her son to the Lord, does it? Sometimes the best part of giving is the joy the giver receives.

The highlight of Hannah's story, however, is recorded in 1 Samuel 2:21: "And the Lord was gracious to Hannah; she gave birth to three sons and two daughters. Meanwhile, the boy Samuel grew up in the presence of the Lord." God gave Hannah five more children after

Samuel. What's more, Samuel, the son she surrendered to the Lord, is still speaking to God's people today while we don't know any of the names of Peninnah's children.

What's God Asking You to Give?

If God is asking you to surrender something to Him before you have it, it is so you will not attempt to shape, control, or minimize what He ultimately wants to do for and through you. You may be at a time in your life when you are facing another barren year, which did not turn out like anything you wanted it to be. Yet you cannot quit or give up, for something in you is asking you to commit your future to the Lord, the future you *hope* to have but for some reason have not seen come to pass. I urge you to do what Hannah did, and then to be encouraged by Hannah's story. Surrender your future to the Lord, follow through on the commitment, worship God, and then watch Him work on your behalf in a way that will astound you.

That is certainly my testimony. God has taken the ministry I surrendered to Him years ago, before I had anything to do, and made it a fruitful work that I love. None of it looks like I thought it would 30 years ago, but God has surpassed all that I could have imagined back then. Therefore, I am not only encouraging you from the biblical story of Hannah, I am encouraging you from my own testimony lessons. God is good and I have found again and again that no one can out-give him, but it sure is fun trying.

MARY
The Annunciation

In this story, let's return to the life of Mary, the mother of Jesus, who we also studied earlier. Some are hesitant to talk much about Mary due to the position some theologians in certain churches have assigned her, but Mary is worthy of our consideration as a woman of purpose, so let's see what we can learn from Mary's life that can help us in our quest for purpose.

The Announcement

Here is the announcement that ushered in the Christmas story:

> In the sixth month of Elizabeth's pregnancy, God sent the angel Gabriel to Nazareth, a town in Galilee, to a virgin pledged to be married to a man named Joseph, a descendant of David. The virgin's name was Mary. The angel went to her and said, "Greetings, you who are highly favored! The Lord is with you." Mary was greatly troubled at his words and wondered what kind of greeting this might be. But the angel said to

her, "Do not be afraid, Mary; you have found favor with God. You will conceive and give birth to a son, and you are to call him Jesus. He will be great and will be called the Son of the Most High. The Lord God will give him the throne of his father David, and he will reign over Jacob's descendants forever; his kingdom will never end."

"How will this be," Mary asked the angel, "since I am a virgin?" The angel answered, "The Holy Spirit will come on you, and the power of the Most High will overshadow you. So the holy one to be born will be called the Son of God. Even Elizabeth your relative is going to have a child in her old age, and she who was said to be unable to conceive is in her sixth month. For no word from God will ever fail." "I am the Lord's servant," Mary answered. "May your word to me be fulfilled." Then the angel left her (Luke 1:26-38).

We don't know much about Mary since this is the first mention of her in the Bible. God decided that Mary was to be the mother of Jesus, however, and sent Gabriel to make the announcement. Put yourself in Mary's place. She was probably a teenager. Perhaps this was her first encounter with a supernatural being. She was engaged, but was informed that she was pregnant by the Holy Spirit. With all that background, Mary asked one question and only one: "How can this be?"

The Answer

The angel gave her a simple answer: "The Holy Spirit will come upon you." Mary had as much information after the question as before, for she did not have an awareness of the Spirit that we have today. All she understood was that God was going to make it happen. It is fascinating that she did not ask another question, but simply responded, "May your word to me be fulfilled." That represents great faith, which is the prerequisite for anyone who wants to find and fulfill his or her purpose. You may think that Mary's purpose was to give birth to Jesus, but it was not. To identify her purpose, we go a little further into Luke's gospel to see the words of Elizabeth, Mary's cousin, that define Mary's purpose: "Blessed is she who has believed that the Lord would fulfill his promises to her!"

It was Mary's role to oversee in faith the promises and mission of her son, Jesus. Mary was there when the shepherds came to see Jesus, when the Magi came to worship Jesus, when Herod came to kill Jesus, when the elders of Israel listened to 12-year-old Jesus, when Jesus began His public ministry, when Jesus was hung on a cross, and when the Holy Spirit was poured out on the day of Pentecost. If Mary's purpose was to give birth to Jesus, her purpose was finished the day He was born. Her purpose to believe God for her Son's protection and blessing was a lifelong task.

The Application

Perhaps you have not progressed in your purpose because you want more information. You have asked "How can this be?" and received the same answer as Mary did: "God will accomplish it." Since that is not specific enough for you, you wait, and wait, and wait, and today you are no further along than you were a few years ago because your expectations are unrealistic. God does not owe you a full explanation before you begin to take steps in your purpose. You continue to wait, and therefore He waits, and you end up staying in precisely the same place you have been in for quite a while, deriving satisfaction that you are waiting on the Lord.

I urge you to reconsider Mary and her role not only in the Christmas story but also in the life of Jesus. Observe her reactions and responses, and apply them to your own life. Your role is not just to give birth to your purpose; your role is to raise it to maturity so it can bear fruit. May God be with you as you trust the Lord every step of the way as you walk out your purpose.

THREE WOMEN
AND A BABY

For the women in this chapter, let's go back to the book of Exodus and look at not one, but three women and their role in the life of one little baby who was eventually given the name of Moses.

Mother and Daughter

> Now a man of the tribe of Levi married a Levite woman, and she became pregnant and gave birth to a son. When she saw that he was a fine child, she hid him for three months. But when she could hide him no longer, she got a papyrus basket for him and coated it with tar and pitch. Then she placed the child in it and put it among the reeds along the bank of the Nile. His sister stood at a distance to see what would happen to him (Exodus 2:1-4).

Moses' mother (the Torah reported that her name was Jochebed) gave birth to her son at a time when Pharaoh had ordered that all male babies be tossed into the Nile River to drown or be eaten by crocodiles. Many mothers complied, but Moses' mother saw that there was something different about her baby—that he was a "fine" or "no ordinary" child. She recognized her baby's purpose and decided to protect him.

When she could not hide him any longer, she finally complied with Pharaoh's decree. She put her child in the Nile, but *first* she built a waterproof basket and placed him in it. That was a creative way to comply with the rule and represented complete trust that God would oversee the purpose she had discovered when she looked in her baby's eyes.

Then the baby's sister, who we assume was Miriam, followed the basket as it floated down the river and got stuck in some reeds along the shore. Why would this young girl follow the basket's progress unless she and her mother believed that something good, something miraculous was going to transpire to save their son and brother? The women did not only put the basket on the river and commit it to the Lord's care; they followed up to see what role they would play in the safe delivery of their faith package.

Princess and Slave

Then Pharaoh's daughter went down to the Nile to bathe, and her attendants were walking along the riverbank. She saw the basket among the reeds and sent her female slave to get it. She opened it and saw the baby. He was crying, and she felt sorry for him. "This is one of the Hebrew babies," she said. Then his sister asked Pharaoh's daughter, "Shall I go and get one of the Hebrew women to nurse the baby for you?" "Yes, go," she answered. So the girl went and got the baby's mother. Pharaoh's daughter said to her, "Take this baby and nurse him for me, and I will pay you." So the woman took the baby and nursed him. When the child grew older, she took him to Pharaoh's daughter and he became her son. She named him Moses, saying, "I drew him out of the water" (Exodus 2:5-10).

Pharaoh's daughter had her slave retrieve the baby when they discovered him as the princess was ready to bathe. God had taken the baby right to royalty's bathtub, so to speak, and had the baby cry on cue so that the princess' sympathies were aroused. Moses' sister was not afraid and revealed herself, offering to find a woman to nurse the baby, and the princess agreed.

Pharaoh's daughter, like the baby's mother, defied the king's order and adopted the baby. Why didn't Pharaoh question where this baby came from? Why didn't one of the slaves report the princess' unusual act to the king? That didn't happen because Moses floated down the river, not on the waters of the Nile, but on his mother's and sister's faith. Their faith coincided with the princess' bathing schedule, their faith caused the baby to cry, and then their faith caused Pharaoh's household to pay Moses' mother to nurse her own child.

Lessons

All three of these women had faith and God used them to carry out His plan to save His people through Moses, their leader and deliverer. While their names were not revealed or preserved, the product of their faith, Moses, is known by countless millions. Perhaps God has empowered you to recognize the purpose of someone else and is asking you to exercise faith that will encourage and nurture that person's destiny? Maybe you will derive your own livelihood from "nursing" the purpose of others, or invest your resources in their care and development? Or are you fearlessly to "follow" the river path of someone else to watch over and speak up for them when they cannot speak for themselves?

These three women changed history because they had faith. I encourage you to have the same kind of faith for those who are closest to you, and watch God fulfill His purpose through them because of you. In their purpose, you may just find your own.

MIRIAM
A Female Leader

In the last profile, we looked at three women of faith who were involved in the life of baby Moses. The first was his mother, named Jochebed; the second was Pharaoh's daughter, who adopted baby Moses; and the third was Miriam, Moses' older sister. We don't hear anything about the first two women after the story of Moses' adoption in Exodus 2:1-10, but we do read more about Miriam, so let's look at what we know.

A Woman of Faith

I pointed earlier that Miriam was a bold young girl full of faith, for she emerged from the reeds along the river to speak with Pharaoh's princess daughter and offer to find a woman to nurse the baby. That took courage and some acting skills, for Miriam had to pretend that she didn't know to whom the baby belonged.

Moses was raised in Pharaoh's household for the next 40 years, then fled into the wilderness for another 40 years before he returned to order the then-ruling Pharaoh to "let My people go." Let's assume that Miriam was 10 years older than Moses, which means she was 90 years old when Moses came back to Egypt to fulfill his purpose of delivering and leading Israel (we see no mention that Miriam was married). We learn in Micah 6:4 that, "I [the Lord] brought you up from the land of Egypt, I redeemed you from the house of bondage; and I sent before you Moses, Aaron, and Miriam." It is commonly said that Moses, or perhaps Moses and Aaron led Israel out of Egypt. Few people include Miriam in a leadership role, but the Lord clearly saw her in one.

When the people of God crossed through the parted Red Sea, they saw Pharaoh's army destroyed by the Sea's waters when they returned to their place. The elderly Miriam is referenced once again, identified as a prophet and a leader:

> When Pharaoh's horses, chariots and horsemen went into the sea, the Lord brought the waters of the sea back over them, but the Israelites walked through the sea on dry ground. *Then Miriam the prophet*, Aaron's sister, took a timbrel in her hand, and all *the women followed her*, with timbrels and dancing. Miriam sang to them: "Sing to the Lord, for he is highly exalted. Both horse and driver he has hurled into the sea" (Exodus 15:19-21, emphasis added).

A Woman of Power

We later learn in Numbers 12 that Miriam was unhappy with Moses' selection of a wife and enlisted Aaron to heap criticism on Moses, perhaps feeling threatened or slighted by their foreign sister-in-law. The Lord summoned the three siblings to His presence where He rebuked Miriam and Aaron. During that encounter, Miriam was smitten with leprosy: "So Miriam was confined outside the camp for seven days, and the people did not move on till she was brought back" (Numbers 12:15). It seems that the people could not move on during her seven-day ordeal, for her leadership and presence were an irreplaceable part of the people of God in the Wilderness.

Miriam was obviously a powerful woman with a significant leadership position, which she misused at one point to try and usurp Moses' position and authority. Nevertheless, she was faithful for many decades and even in her wayward moment became an example to God's people of how *not* to act, as well as a recipient of God's grace that restored her: "In cases of defiling skin diseases, be very careful to do exactly as the Levitical priests instruct you. You must follow carefully what I have commanded them. Remember what the Lord your God did to Miriam along the way after you came out of Egypt" (Deuteronomy 24:8-9).

God expects women of purpose to function in their assignment, and that assignment may bring them into leadership. When they lead, they are held to the same standard as anyone else and are to use their leadership power to serve others, not to seek more power or authority. Have you held back from expressing your purpose because you were ambivalent about your gender?

If so, I urge you to consider Miriam and accept your purpose. If you know a woman who has done this, encourage that woman who is holding back with that issue. God is not nearly as "hung up" on the gender issue as some of His people are, and He will continue to equip women with gifts and purpose. It is up to those women to accept God's assignment, and it is up to those around them to accept the fact that God will indeed choose and empower women of purpose to do His will and lead His people.

DORCAS
Always Doing Good

It is time to discuss one of my favorite examples of purpose in the Bible. It is the story of a woman who was not well connected, did not have money or power, and did not touch hundreds of lives. She simply had a heart for the poor and the ability to sew, and she combined those two things into one of the more remarkable purpose expressions in God's word. Her name was Tabitha or Dorcas, and here is her story:

> In Joppa there was a disciple named Tabitha (which, when translated, is Dorcas), who was always doing good and helping the poor. About that time she became sick and died, and her body was washed and placed in an upstairs room. Lydda was near Joppa; so when the disciples heard that Peter was in Lydda, they sent two men to him and urged him, "Please come at once!" Peter went with them, and when he arrived he was taken upstairs to the room. All the widows stood around him, crying and showing him the robes and other clothing that

Dorcas had made while she was still with them. Peter sent them all out of the room; then he got down on his knees and prayed. Turning toward the dead woman, he said, "Tabitha, get up." She opened her eyes, and seeing Peter she sat up. He took her by the hand and helped her to her feet. Then he called the believers and the widows and presented her to them alive. This became known all over Joppa, and many people believed in the Lord (Acts 9:36-42).

A Closer Look

If you are like me, you probably focused on Peter when you read the above passage. When I began teaching about purpose, I made Dorcas the focus. If Dorcas was alive today, she would have a sewing machine, a source for cloth and thread, and a heart to sew for the poor. She was a "nothing" woman—she had no prestige or position—in a "nowhere" village who was helping "nobody" people. Dorcas had *nothing* going for her except she was a woman of purpose, always doing good and helping the poor. Therefore, in reality she had *everything* going for her.

When she walked through her village, she saw the same people everyone else saw, but she viewed them through the eyes of purpose. She saw poor women who needed clothing. Your purpose sensitizes you to things around you that you think *everyone* should or can see, but they cannot. You see them because it is part of who God made you to be. If you think or say, "Why doesn't someone do something about what I see?", you don't understand that they *cannot* do something because they cannot *see* what you see. *You* are the somebody who needs to do something.

Dorcas took it upon herself to help her neighbors and obviously became an important part of her community. When Dorcas passed away, those neighbors she helped were sad and felt the loss. In her day of trouble, however, when Dorcas could not cry out on her own behalf, the evidence of a life yielded to God's purpose cried out for her.

Peter, the most significant spiritual leader in the world at the time, broke off what he was doing to come down and view her dead body. He was so moved both by how much everyone missed Dorcas and by the impact she had made while she was alive that he brought her back from the dead to continue her work. Once that happened, a revival broke out in Dorcas' village and she didn't have to preach a message. Her sermon was a life full of purpose when she did good deeds for poor people. What an amazing story.

The Lessons

Do you see any needs around you that you can meet like Dorcas did? If you do, what are you waiting for? Go meet them. Are you hung up on what you don't have and what you can't do? Then start focusing on what you *do* have and *can* do. Have you convinced yourself that you can't make a difference in the world around you, or have you chosen not to make that difference? Either way, your thinking is wrong. The only reason you can't is that you have told yourself you can't and it has become a self-fulfilling prophecy.

Please take the lessons from Dorcas' life to heart and follow her example. When you do, you have all of heaven's attention, no matter how trivial or insignificant what you are doing seems to be. It's time to stop examining what you *don't* have and consider what you *do* have, and that is a purpose that no one else can perform like you. What's more, when you flow in your purpose, God flows with you, so you are in the purpose business with God as your partner.

It's time that you answer a difficult and challenging question: When you leave, will people miss you like they missed Dorcas? The only way you will be able to answer yes is to start fulfilling your purpose today, right now, where you are, with what you have.

PRISCILLA
Working with Her Husband

Our next purpose profile is of a woman who was never named in the Bible apart from her husband, but was always mentioned first and appeared to be an equal to her husband as they taught, traveled, and pastored. Her name was Priscilla and her husband's name was Aquila. Let's look at what we know about this woman.

The Introduction

We first meet Priscilla in Luke's Acts 18 account:

After this, Paul left Athens and went to Corinth. There he met a Jew named Aquila, a native of Pontus, who had recently come from Italy with his wife Priscilla, because Claudius had ordered all Jews to leave Rome. Paul went to see them, and because he was a tentmaker as they were, he stayed and worked with them (1-3).

After Paul got to know this couple, Luke reported,

Paul stayed on in Corinth for some time. Then he left the brothers and sisters and sailed for Syria, accompanied by Priscilla and Aquila.

Before he sailed, he had his hair cut off at Cenchreae because of a vow he had taken. They arrived at Ephesus, where Paul left Priscilla and Aquila (Acts 18:18-19).

Priscilla and Aquila then made a major contribution by equipping a powerful minister named Apollos who needed more depth of understanding about the Way:

He [Apollos] began to speak boldly in the synagogue. When Priscilla and Aquila heard him, they invited him to their home and explained to him the way of God more adequately (Acts 18:26).

Luke made it clear that Aquila was not a man who was supported by his wife. No, this was a ministry team and when Luke thought of them, he (as well as Paul) listed them together with Priscilla's name mentioned first. That is quite a statement about her worth and anointing in ministry, but there's more.

The Endorsement

Paul wrote his letter to the Romans and had this to say about Priscilla and Aquila: "Greet Priscilla and Aquila, my co-workers in Christ Jesus. They risked their lives for me. Not only I but all the churches of the Gentiles are grateful to them. Greet also the church that meets at their house" (Romans 16:3-5).

Paul stated that Priscilla was his co-worker who he trusted to pastor, teach, and lead the believers wherever she and her husband were, which included Corinth, Ephesus, and Rome (that also made them missionaries). When Paul wrote to the Corinthians and to Timothy, he mentioned the married team: "The churches in the province of Asia send you greetings. Aquila and Priscilla greet you warmly in the Lord, and so does the church that meets at their house" (1 Corinthians 16:19), and "Greet Priscilla and Aquila and the household of Onesiphorus" (2 Timothy 4:19).

Priscilla was a valued asset to Paul's Kingdom work as was her husband. He saw them both as effective ministers and was not including Priscilla as a concession to Aquila. Her ministry was not endorsed simply because she was married to Aquila; her ministry was sanctioned because God had gifted her. If God had gifted her, then no one had the right to diminish her call simply because she was a woman.

The Lesson

The Church has tried to do its work with one arm tied behind its back when it has attempted to limit or ignore women with Holy Spirit gifts. The same can be said for many other walks of life like business, academics, and politics. The answer is not to launch a feminist movement so that women in general can be promoted or recognized. The answer is to treat women as men are treated: Examine their lives for purpose and gifts and then equip and empower them to operate as God intended.

The lesson we learn from Priscilla is not that every woman married to a man in ministry should be his co-worker in that ministry. That should only happen when she is gifted to do so. When she is, however, she should be recognized, honored, and utilized as such. When she is not, then she should be released to the purpose God has for her, and equipped by the church for success.

If you are a woman, are you shying away from a role God has for you? Are you trying to embrace one He does not have for you? If you are a man, do you recognize women as equals when God has gifted them to do what you do? Are you empowering women where you work or minister without bias or envy? As you ponder these questions and others that this book may have raised in your mind, you will help to release the gifts God chose to bestow on women and thus empower the church to utilize all His servants as they express God's purpose.

MARY MAGDALENE
Closer than a Brother

There is a woman who is named more than a dozen times in all four of the gospels, who knew and traveled with Jesus, and who ended up remaining closer to Him than any of His brothers or disciples, except John. She was brave, determined, and loyal, and she received special insight from God as a reward for her courage and tenacity. Her name was Mary Magdalene.

What Do We Know?

We know that Mary was from the Galilee area north of Samaria, which was Jesus' chosen base for His public ministry. At some point, Mary had an encounter with Jesus and was healed and set free as Luke described:

> After this, Jesus traveled about from one town and village to another, proclaiming the good news of the kingdom of God. The Twelve were with him, and also some women who had been cured of evil spirits and diseases: Mary (called Magdalene) from whom seven demons had come out; Joanna the wife of Chuza, the

manager of Herod's household; Susanna; and many others. These women were helping to support them out of their own means (Luke 8:1–3).

When Mary was set free, she became one of the women who traveled with Jesus and ministered to His needs as well as those of His disciples. We cannot overlook how radical this must have been to have a group of women traveling with the disciples who were not their wives.

Whenever Mary Magdalene is listed with other women in the gospels, she is always listed first (except when she was with Mary, the mother of Jesus), which probably indicates that she was a take-charge person who also had some means from which she helped to financially support Jesus:

- Mary Magdalene and the other Mary were sitting there opposite the tomb (Matthew 27:61).

- After the Sabbath, at dawn on the first day of the week, Mary Magdalene and the other Mary went to look at the tomb (Matthew 28:1).

- It was Mary Magdalene, Joanna, Mary the mother of James, and the others with them who told this to the apostles (Luke 24:10).

- Near the cross of Jesus stood his mother, his mother's sister, Mary the wife of Clopas, and Mary Magdalene (John 19:25).

Mary is most prominently featured in the accounts of Jesus' death and resurrection, however, and it was there that she distinguished herself as a faithful and fearless servant and disciple, whom women and men would do well to emulate.

Close By

The gospels tell us that Mary was close at hand during Jesus' trial, His death march through Jerusalem, His crucifixion, and His death. Mary noted where they buried Jesus but being a good Jew, she went home for the Sabbath and then came back the next day with at least one other woman to anoint Jesus' body for burial. It is John that included the most detail about Mary's activities at the tomb:

> Now Mary stood outside the tomb crying. As she wept, she bent over to look into the tomb and saw two angels in white, seated where Jesus' body had been, one at the head and the other at the foot.
>
> They asked her, "Woman, why are you crying?" "They have taken my Lord away," she said, "and I don't know where they have put him." At this, she turned around and saw Jesus standing there, but she did not realize that it was Jesus. He asked her, "Woman, why are you crying? Who is it you are looking for?" Thinking he was the gardener, she said, "Sir, if you have carried him away, tell me where you have put him, and I will get him." Jesus said to her, "Mary." She turned toward him and cried out in Aramaic, "Rabboni!" (which means "Teacher").
>
> Jesus said, "Do not hold on to me, for I have not yet ascended to the Father. Go instead to my brothers and tell them, 'I am ascending to my Father and your Father, to my God and your God.'" Mary Magdalene went to the disciples

with the news: "I have seen the Lord!" And she told them that he had said these things to her (John 20:11-18).

Notice that Mary referred to Jesus not as *the* Lord, but *my* Lord. She was heartbroken, but she was determined to be loyal to Jesus even after what she thought was the end, and she was rewarded with being the first to know that Jesus had come back to life as He had promised.

The Lesson

Mary, equipped with a revelation of the risen Jesus, went back to the disciples to tell them the good news, but they did not believe her right away. Peter and John went running to the tomb, found it as Mary had reported, and then went home. Not Mary. She stayed at the tomb, weeping and mourning because she did not know where Jesus' body was and was thus unable to complete the task she came to perform. It was then that Jesus revealed Himself to her by calling her by name, and once again she went back to the brothers to report what she had seen and heard.

Mary instructed these men (dare we say *led* these men) because she *knew* Jesus, *followed* Jesus, was *close* to Jesus, *heard* His voice, and had a *personal revelation of truth* from Jesus Himself. That qualified her to teach and lead, and when all was said and done, that revelation was all she needed to serve Jesus and others effectively. The men dismissed her because they didn't believe what Mary reported and didn't accept that a woman could teach them much of anything. Does that sound like the Church through the ages, even today?

If you are a woman and identify with or resemble Mary, you have undoubtedly learned something from Jesus that isn't just for other women, it is for everyone. If

Jesus was willing to reveal Himself to you, knowing you are a woman—if it didn't matter to Him that you are a woman—then why should it matter to you or anyone else?

Mary fulfilled the proverb that states "there is a friend who sticks closer than a brother" (Proverbs 18:24). Who said that person who is close had to be a man? If you are a woman, I urge you to stay close to Jesus and listen and obey when He calls your name. If you are a man, I encourage you to listen to the women in your life who are close to Jesus, and hopefully they will share with you what Jesus has told them—just like Mary Magdalene did.

THE WOMEN AT ROME

In this chapter, we will look at a list of women the Apostle Paul mentioned as he closed his epistle to the Romans. We will then focus on two of the women named Phoebe and Junia to learn what role they had in the early church

The List

When we read Romans 16:1-9, Paul mentioned nine women who were involved in the Roman church. They were Phoebe, Priscilla, Mary, Junia, Tryphena, Tryphosa, Persis, Rufus' mother, and Nereus' sister. In addition, Paul wrote in 16:11, "I urge you, brothers and *sisters*, to watch out for those who cause divisions and put obstacles in your way that are contrary to the teaching you have learned. Keep away from them" (emphasis added). Paul was not only writing to the men, he was addressing the women as equals.

From the list of nine, we can conclude that women played an important role in either establishing or maintaining the church in Rome, which had become significant due to its location. Rome was the capital of the Empire and a crossroads for everything that Rome stood for and cherished. It was also a meeting place for the people of the Empire who had official business.

Women played an important role in the church and Paul acknowledged what they did. Priscilla had risked her life for Paul and she led a church in her home along with her husband. Mary worked hard for the Romans saints. Tryphena, Tryphosa, and Persis were also commended for their hard work, presumably in the church. What work goes on in the church except for evangelism, discipleship, pastoral duties, care for the poor, preaching, and teaching? These women must have been involved in some of or all those activities, sharing the leadership roles in the church with their male counterparts.

Two women stand out in the list among Paul's comments, however, and they are Phoebe and Junia. Let's look at them apart from the others.

A Deacon and an Apostle

> I commend to you our sister Phoebe, a deacon of the church in Cenchreae. I ask you to receive her in the Lord in a way worthy of his people and to give her any help she may need from you, for she has been the benefactor of many people, including me (Romans 16:1-2).

Phoebe had served in the church at Cenchreae, a town close to Corinth. She distinguished herself to such an extent that Paul entrusted his letter to the Romans to her for delivery, instructing the church to provide whatever she needed. Phoebe was a deacon or servant and recognized for her exceptional work with a special mention in Paul's letter. She was traveling just like any man in ministry, and Paul had no reservations about her role or travels.

Then there is the woman Junia: "Greet Andronicus and Junia, my fellow Jews who have been in prison with me. They are outstanding among the apostles, and they were in Christ before I was" (Romans 16:7). There is some disagreement over who Junia was or if she was even a woman. The name Junia has also been transcribed as Junias, which appears to have been a female or male name. We assume Adronicus was her husband, but he could have been her sibling or brother in the Lord.

Then there is Paul's commendation, which included the words "outstanding among the apostles." That could mean that Junia was well known among the apostles for her contributions to the ministry team. It could also mean that she was an apostle herself. She came to the Lord before Paul, and was imprisoned along with Paul and Adronicus because of her work for the Lord, which leads me to believe that she was more than just a companion. She was a co-worker.

The Romans would not have imprisoned a spouse unless she was a nuisance as the male workers had become to Rome. The historic church considered Junia a woman and an apostle, so this assumption of her apostolic role has more than a little credibility.

The Lesson

Paul gave us two examples of women of purpose who were leaders in the early church, one a deacon and the other an apostle. They had spiritual gifts that distinguished them from their peers. If Paul did not quibble over their gender, and made no qualifying statements that would have caused the church to treat them differently than the men, then we should be careful not to do the same in their case or in the case of present-day women who also serve, teach, preach, or stand out for their work in the church and among God's people.

Paul set out the requirements for women in ministry when he addressed the requirements for leadership in 1 Timothy 3:8-11:

> In the same way, deacons are to be worthy of respect, sincere, not indulging in much wine, and not pursuing dishonest gain. They must keep hold of the deep truths of the faith with a clear conscience. They must first be tested; and then if there is nothing against them, let them serve as deacons. In the same way, the women are to be worthy of respect, not malicious talkers but temperate and trustworthy in everything.

Paul had a large task and purpose, which was to establish the Church among the Gentiles. He could not do this without using *all* the gifted people at his disposal, and some of them were women. The same strategy should be employed today. There are no rules that say a certain number or percentage in leadership must be women, but there are no rules to say that they cannot serve, if their purpose and gifts are proven to benefit God's cause.

I am certain that there are many women like Junia and Phoebe who are serving in the Church, with many more waiting in the wings. Let's not hinder them but make room in our hearts and ministries for women whom God has chosen to call and take their place alongside men.

ABIGAIL
The Intercessor

The more I searched the Bible, the more women of purpose I noticed to include in this bool. In this chapter, let's examine a remarkable woman whose purpose of intercession saved her life, the lives of her servants, and her worthless husband. Her name was Abigail and her story is found in 1 Samuel 25, which I would advise you to read before you proceed.

A Noble Woman

When Abigail's surly and nasty husband, Nabal, insulted David's men who had come for supplies in return for the protective services they had rendered, Abigail heard about it through one of the servants. This tells us that she could be trusted with people's secrets and listened to those around her who were more in touch with what was going on. Once she heard what Nabal had done, Abigail knew she had to act quickly, so she assembled some provisions and set off intercept David before he sought his revenge against Nabal. While her husband was incapable of leadership, Abigail arose and led in his place.

When Abigail saw David, she humbled herself,

falling prostrate at his feet and begging for mercy because of her husband's foolish behavior. She showed herself humble, wise, and spiritual, for she framed her remarks in the context of what God had promised to do in David's life:

> "Please forgive your servant's presumption. The Lord your God will certainly make a lasting dynasty for my lord, because you fight the Lord's battles, and no wrongdoing will be found in you as long as you live. Even though someone is pursuing you to take your life, the life of my lord will be bound securely in the bundle of the living by the Lord your God, but the lives of your enemies he will hurl away as from the pocket of a sling. When the Lord has fulfilled for my lord every good thing he promised concerning him and has appointed him ruler over Israel, my lord will not have on his conscience the staggering burden of needless bloodshed or of having avenged himself. And when the Lord your God has brought my lord success, remember your servant" (1 Samuel 25:28-32).

In addition to all her outstanding traits, Abigail was also a woman of faith. She trusted that the Lord would do for David all He promised He would do, and asked David to remember her on that day. David admitted that Abigail prevented him from carrying out his anger and received her gifts—but that's not all he did.

Her Promotion

Because Abigail interceded on behalf of both Nabal and David, God interceded on her behalf as well:

> Then in the morning, when Nabal was sober,

his wife told him all these things, and his heart failed him and he became like a stone. About ten days later, the Lord struck Nabal and he died. When David heard that Nabal was dead, he said, "Praise be to the Lord, who has upheld my cause against Nabal for treating me with contempt. He has kept his servant from doing wrong and has brought Nabal's wrongdoing down on his own head." Then David sent word to Abigail, asking her to become his wife. His servants went to Carmel and said to Abigail, "David has sent us to you to take you to become his wife." She bowed down with her face to the ground and said, "I am your servant and am ready to serve you and wash the feet of my lord's servants." Abigail quickly got on a donkey and, attended by her five female servants, went with David's messengers and became his wife (1 Samuel 25:37-42).

I hope this was not the last time that David consulted Abigail for spiritual advice, and I also hope it was not the last time she took it upon herself to intercede according to the insight and wisdom she had. Regardless of those hopes, Abigail distinguished herself as a woman of purpose, who set an example for all women—all believers for that matter—of courageous intercession.

What insight has God given you about circumstances around you? Are you taking it upon yourself to lead the way out? Are you talking with those in power to help peacefully resolve the situation? Are you talking to the Lord, making your petitions known to Him? You don't have to have a title to lead, and you should not shrink back from leading because of gender. Be true to who God made you to be, and let God fight your battles as you step out according to the insight you have, just like Abigail did.

NAOMI AND RUTH
A Dynamic Team

In this chapter, let's look at two women whose purpose was woven together into one. The book of Ruth is beautifully-written, even though God is only indirectly referred to throughout the narrative. Even so, His "fingerprints" are everywhere in the story. The book is named after Ruth, but could just as easily have been named after her mother-in-law, Naomi. Let's look at their purpose story now.

The Background

Naomi, her husband, and her two sons left Israel due to a famine and went to the land of Moab where the two sons married two local girls, Orpah and Ruth. Some time later, their father died and then the two sons died, leaving Naomi a widow with no sons or grandchildren (some have called her the female Job of the Old Testament). Eventually, Naomi decided to return to Israel where she would face a hard life as a widow with no men to support her. She urged her daughters-in-law to stay behind to fend for themselves. Orpah reluctantly did so, but Ruth uttered words that we have often used in wedding ceremony vows:

But Ruth replied, "Don't urge me to leave you or to turn back from you. Where you go I will go, and where you stay I will stay. Your people will be my people and your God my God. Where you die I will die, and there I will be buried. May the Lord deal with me, be it ever so severely, if even death separates you and me." When Naomi realized that Ruth was determined to go with her, she stopped urging her (Ruth 1:16–18).

Ruth proclaimed her loyalty to Naomi, and the women made their way back to Israel but before they did, Naomi changed her name:

"Don't call me Naomi," she told them. "Call me Mara, because the Almighty has made my life very bitter. I went away full, but the Lord has brought me back empty. Why call me Naomi? The Lord has afflicted me; the Almighty has brought misfortune upon me" (Ruth 1:20–21).

The Breakthrough

When the women returned to Israel, they had no source of income, so Ruth went to work harvesting barley, and that is when the Lord began to work out everything according to a grand master plan that is breathtaking to behold. Ruth just happened to work in a field owned by a man named Boaz who was Naomi's husband's relative. According to Old Testament law, that relative, called a kinsman redeemer, had to marry Ruth and provide for her. It turns out Boaz was already attracted to Ruth because of her reputation:

"I've been told all about what you have done

for your mother-in-law since the death of your husband—how you left your father and mother and your homeland and came to live with a people you did not know before. May the Lord repay you for what you have done. May you be richly rewarded by the Lord, the God of Israel, under whose wings you have come to take refuge" (Ruth 2:11-12).

Naomi coached Ruth through what she should do once she had Boaz's attention, and Ruth was obedient, which impressed Boaz once again:

"The Lord bless you, my daughter," he replied. "This kindness is greater than that which you showed earlier: You have not run after the younger men, whether rich or poor. And now, my daughter, don't be afraid. I will do for you all you ask. All the people of my town know that you are a woman of noble character. Although it is true that I am a guardian-redeemer of our family, there is another who is more closely related than I. Stay here for the night, and in the morning if he wants to do his duty as your guardian-redeemer, good; let him redeem you. But if he is not willing, as surely as the Lord lives I will do it. Lie here until morning" (Ruth 3:10-13).

The Blessing

It was not only Boaz who was impressed with Ruth; her exceptional qualities captured God's attention as well. Boaz married her as he promised and they had a son, who also turned out to be a blessing to Naomi, his grandmother: "Then Naomi took the child in her arms and cared for him. The women living there said, 'Naomi has a son!' And they named him Obed. He was the father of Jesse, the father of David" (Ruth 4:16-17). God not only provided for Ruth but bestowed on her a great honor, for she became the great-grandmother to King David. Ruth from Moab, which was an enemy of Israel, became part of Jesus' family tree. As a bonus, Naomi, who had changed her name to "bitter," had her joy, hope, and legacy restored. God is good.

Women don't have to preach, lead a business, or write songs sung by many for God to use them—Ruth is proof of that. Are you faithfully serving the members of your family or another person close to you, but it doesn't seem like anyone is watching or paying attention? If so, then Ruth's example should encourage you to stay the course. Ruth was loyal to one woman, but because she was, she had many admirers, and God was one of them. He not only took care of her, but He also blessed her with offspring who are still blessing God's people today. God knows how to open doors for both men and women, and He has a door with a blessing behind it for you. Armed with that knowledge, I trust you will be encouraged to serve the Lord where you are, realizing that even if no one else is watching, He is.

RAHAB
A Controversial Figure

The playwright Oscar Wilde once said, "Every saint has a past, every sinner has a future." That is certainly true for the woman we will look at in this chapter. She is an Old Testament character who is mentioned three times in the New Testament, and her occupation has made her somewhat of a controversial figure. Her name is Rahab.

The New Testament

What does the New Testament say about Rahab? The writer of Hebrews wrote, "By faith the prostitute Rahab, because she welcomed the spies, was not killed with those who were disobedient" (Hebrews 11:31). Then James wrote,

> You see that a person is considered righteous by what they do and not by faith alone. In the same way, was not even Rahab the prostitute considered righteous for what she did when she gave lodging to the spies and sent them off in a different direction? As the body without the spirit is dead, so faith without deeds is dead (James 2:24-26).

What's more surprising is the third mention of Rahab, this time in Matthew's gospel as he outlined Jesus' family tree: "Salmon the father of Boaz, whose mother was Rahab, Boaz the father of Obed, whose mother was Ruth, Obed the father of Jesse, and Jesse the father of King David" (Matthew 1:5-6).

What do these three passages tell us? First, Rahab was a woman of faith, and both James and Hebrews bear witness to that fact. Those two books also indicate that Rahab was a harlot, but chances are, she ran a hotel of sorts that served as both a boarding house and a place for women to work their trade as ladies of the night.

Who better to know what was going on in the land than someone who ran a hotel and heard all kinds of stories of what was happening from all around the region? Rahab did indeed hear about the Lord and His works on behalf of His people, and those stories stuck in Rahab's mind and heart. When the spies showed up at her establishment one day, she knew what she had to do to save herself and her family.

The Old Testament

Rahab hid the spies whom Joshua had sent out as scouts, and the mayor of Jericho, assuming they would be staying at her establishment, asked her to turn them over to the local officials. Rahab refused, hiding the spies on her roof while saying they had already departed. The locals believed her and left, so then Rahab lowered the spies from her roof. Before they left, however, she negotiated a deal with them in return for her protective services, something she was accustomed to doing in her line of work (negotiate a deal with men, that is):

Before the spies lay down for the night, she

went up on the roof and said to them, "I know that the Lord has given you this land and that a great fear of you has fallen on us, so that all who live in this country are melting in fear because of you. We have heard how the Lord dried up the water of the Red Sea for you when you came out of Egypt, and what you did to Sihon and Og, the two kings of the Amorites east of the Jordan, whom you completely destroyed. When we heard of it, our hearts melted in fear and everyone's courage failed because of you, for the Lord your God is God in heaven above and on the earth below.

"Now then, please swear to me by the Lord that you will show kindness to my family, because I have shown kindness to you. Give me a sure sign that you will spare the lives of my father and mother, my brothers and sisters, and all who belong to them—and that you will save us from death" (Joshua 2:8-13).

The spies agreed to her terms but only if she displayed a scarlet rope from her home when they attacked the city. If they could see the rope, they promised to spare her and her family.

Faith's Reward

When Jericho's walls fell and Joshua attacked, Israel kept its promise and spared her household: "But Joshua spared Rahab the prostitute, with her family and all who belonged to her, because she hid the men Joshua had sent as spies to Jericho—and she lives among the Israelites to this day" (Joshua 6:25). Not only did Rahab live among the Israelites after that, she married and had children, becoming part of King David's and Jesus' family heritage.

Rahab put her faith in the God of Israel and the God of Israel saved her and her kin. I mentioned in the first paragraph that she is controversial because of what she did for a living but there is another reason, which was her deception, dare I say her lies about the men's whereabouts, that saved the spies. It's as if the New Testament anticipated some people's misgivings toward her and endorsed her not once, but twice, for the faith she exercised.

If Rahab could exercise faith and please God, then you should be able to so as well. The message of Rahab is that your past sins and your present occupation cannot keep you from purpose if your heart is set on serving the Lord's will for your life. You don't have to be perfect to be a person of purpose, and when you accept your purpose, God can fashion another future for you that isn't related to who you have been up to this point in time. All you must do is put your trust in Him and He will take care of the rest, so long as you continue to have faith. May the Spirit who helped Rahab help you seek to break with your past and present to embrace a future of purpose.

SARAH
God's Princess

In this chapter, let's look at Sarah, Abraham's wife, another woman of purpose in the Bible. I was not sure whether to include Sarah, for she is not a woman who has drawn a great deal of attention. I don't believe I have ever heard a message preached or read an article written about the lessons to learn from Sarah's life. Perhaps the same is true for you. After reading this chapter, however, you won't be able to say *never*, for I am going to write about this woman of purpose and explain why I finally decided to include her in this book.

The Not-So-Good

Because Abraham is a central figure in the book of Genesis, we also get to know a little about Sarai, which was her birth name. There are a few instances where Sarai made decisions whose repercussions are still being felt in the Middle East today.

1. **A surrogate mother**. Sarai was the one who suggested that Abraham sleep with her maid Hagar so the maid could conceive and give

Abraham and Sarai a child. I won't go into the ancient custom that allowed this practice, but it did not work out well for any of those involved:

> He [Abraham] slept with Hagar, and she conceived. When she knew she was pregnant, she began to despise her mistress. Then Sarai said to Abram, "You are responsible for the wrong I am suffering. I put my slave in your arms, and now that she knows she is pregnant, she despises me. May the Lord judge between you and me." "Your slave is in your hands," Abram said. "Do with her whatever you think best." Then Sarai mistreated Hagar; so she fled from her (Genesis 16:4-6).

2. **Laughter and a lie.** After Hagar's son, Ishmael, was born, the Lord appeared to Abram and changed his name to Abraham and Sarai's name to Sarah (see Genesis 17). The Lord promised that a child would be born to Abraham and Sarah in their old age. Then three visitors came to visit Abraham when he was 99 and Sarah was 90 to report that God's promise was to be fulfilled and Sarah would become pregnant. When Sarah overheard this, she found it humorous:

> So Sarah laughed to herself as she thought, "After I am worn out and my lord is old, will I now have this pleasure?" Then the Lord said to Abraham, "Why did Sarah laugh and say, 'Will I really have a child, now that I am old?' Is anything too hard for the Lord? I will return to

you at the appointed time next year, and Sarah will have a son." Sarah was afraid, so she lied and said, "I did not laugh." But he said, "Yes, you did laugh" (Genesis 18:18:12-15).

3. **Ishmael's eviction.** After Isaac was born, Sarah decided that it was time for Hagar and Abraham's son, Ishmael, to go: "But Sarah saw that the son whom Hagar the Egyptian had borne to Abraham was mocking, And she said to Abraham, 'Get rid of that slave woman and her son, for that woman's son will never share in the inheritance with my son Isaac'" (Genesis 21:9-10).

Now you understand why I was ambivalent about including Sarah in this series, but then I considered all the evidence that qualified Sarah to be a woman of purpose and found enough to warrant her inclusion. Let's look at that evidence now.

The Good

Here is why Sarah is more than worthy to be discussed with other women of purpose.

1. **She was a woman of faith**. We read in Hebrews 11:11-12: "And by faith even Sarah, who was past childbearing age, was enabled to bear children because she considered him faithful who had made the promise. And so from this one man, and he as good as dead, came descendants as numerous as the stars in the sky and as countless as the sand on the seashore." Sarah is the first woman mentioned in the Hebrews 11 list of faith champions. Even though she

laughed but denied it, she had faith and with faith, it is possible to please God. This 90-year-old woman believed God's word that she would yet give birth.

2. **She was submissive**. Abram heard the Lord and left his homeland of Ur to travel by faith to the land God promised him, and Sarai followed him. On two occasions, Abraham lied about who Sarah really was since he was afraid the locals would kill him and take Sarah because she was beautiful. In truth, Sarah was also Abraham's half-sister, which is how he introduced her, conveniently concealing the fact that she was also his wife. How did Sarah react? Peter told us in his first epistle: "For this is the way the holy women of the past who put their hope in God used to adorn themselves. They submitted themselves to their own husbands, like Sarah, who obeyed Abraham and called him her lord. You are her daughters if you do what is right and do not give way to fear" (1 Peter 3:5-6).

3. **She had a sense of humor**. After she was confronted about her laughter and caught in her lie, Sarah memorialized her faults. She named her son Isaac, which meant laughter, explaining, "'God has brought me laughter, and everyone who hears about this will laugh with me.' And she added, 'Who would have said to Abraham that Sarah would nurse children? Yet I have borne him a son in his old age'" (Genesis 21:6-7).

4. **She was God's princess**. God changed

Abram's name, which meant *exalted father*, to Abraham, *faith of a multitude*. God changed Sarai's name, which meant my princess, to Sarah, which meant *mother of nations*: "God also said to Abraham, "As for Sarai your wife, you are no longer to call her Sarai; her name will be Sarah. I will bless her and will surely give you a son by her. I will bless her so that she will be the mother of nations; kings of peoples will come from her'" (Genesis 17:15-16). God identified Sarah as His princess who would play a significant role in His future plans, and anyone whom God honors like that deserves to be considered a woman of purpose.

The Lessons

The obvious lesson from Sarah's story is that your flaws do not disqualify you from a life of purpose just as hers did not. They also don't prevent you from exercising faith for your purpose, which always pleases God. Even though she was unkind to Hagar, even though she laughed and lied about it, God saw Sarah as His princess and changed her name so that others would recognize the fact that He honored her as well.

You have strengths and weaknesses and, if you are like most people, you tend to underestimate your strengths and overemphasize your weaknesses, feeling they disqualify you from an effective and purposeful life. I urge you to consider Sarah, God's princess, the next time you think your failures or flaws are sufficient to render you useless where God's purpose for you is concerned.

MARY AND MARTHA
Purpose Sisters

It's time to look at two sisters who broke all the stereotypes of how women in Israel were expected to act and relate to the Lord. Their names were Mary and Martha and their brother was Lazarus. Neither appears to have been married or mothers of children, but they kept a home with their brother a few miles from Jerusalem. There are three stories that involve the sisters, so let's look at those stories to see what we can learn.

Mary

Here is the first account and it is the best known of the three:

> As Jesus and his disciples were on their way, he came to a village where a woman named Martha opened her home to him. She had a sister called Mary, who sat at the Lord's feet listening to what he said. But Martha was distracted by all the preparations that had to be made. She came to him and asked, "Lord, don't you care that my sister has left me to do the

work by myself? Tell her to help me!" "Martha, Martha," the Lord answered, "you are worried and upset about many things, but few things are needed—or indeed only one. Mary has chosen what is better, and it will not be taken away from her" (Luke 10:38-42).

Most interpretations of this story depict Martha as a busy worrywart who didn't spend time with Jesus because she was concerned with worldly or daily, practical things. That is true in part, but is not the most important lesson of the story. If today you visit the Western or Wailing Wall in Jerusalem, you will find it is a segregated wall. There is a fence and to the right of it stand the women, while the men go to the left side, which includes not only the Wall, but a synagogue prayer area out of view that is even closer to where the Holy of Holies was located.

Mary crossed the fence, so to speak, and had the audacity to sit at Jesus' feet, in effect saying, "I have as much right to sit and listen to Jesus as any man does." Martha was not only bothered that Mary wasn't helping with dinner preparations, she was also upset that she was stepping outside of cultural norms to do what had never been done, which was a woman establishing a teaching relationship with a Jewish rabbi. Jesus endorsed Mary's decision and invited Martha and all women to do the same.

Martha

Martha is always portrayed negatively in the first story, but let's look at the second account where Martha is the one who is sitting at the feet of Jesus, so to speak:

On his arrival, Jesus found that Lazarus had already been in the tomb for four days. Now Bethany was less than two miles from Jerusalem, and many Jews had come to Martha and Mary to comfort them in the loss of their brother. When Martha heard that Jesus was coming, she went out to meet him, but Mary stayed at home.

"Lord," Martha said to Jesus, "if you had been here, my brother would not have died. But I know that even now God will give you whatever you ask." Jesus said to her, "Your brother will rise again." Martha answered, "I know he will rise again in the resurrection at the last day." Jesus said to her, "I am the resurrection and the life. The one who believes in me will live, even though they die; and whoever lives by believing in me will never die. Do you believe this?" "Yes, Lord," she replied, "I believe that you are the Messiah, the Son of God, who is to come into the world."

After she had said this, she went back and called her sister Mary aside. "The Teacher is here," she said, "and is asking for you." When Mary heard this, she got up quickly and went to him. Now Jesus had not yet entered the village, but was still at the place where Martha had met him. When the Jews who had been with Mary in the house, comforting her, noticed how quickly she got up and went out, they followed her, supposing she was going to the tomb to mourn there. When Mary reached the place where Jesus was and saw him, she fell at his feet and said, "Lord, if you had been here, my brother would not have died" (John 11:17-32).

Mary stayed at home when she heard Jesus was in

town. Perhaps she was angry with Jesus that He had not come to save her brother, or maybe she was too distraught to get up. Either way, it was Martha who talked with Jesus, and what a discussion it was. Martha revealed that she may have been busy in the kitchen, but she had been listening. She knew Jesus was the Messiah and the Son of God (Jesus told Peter that the Father revealed that insight to him, so the Father had to reveal it to Martha). She knew that her brother would rise again at the resurrection of the dead. She also declared that she had faith but admitted that she didn't understand why Jesus had delayed coming. She was honest but she still put her trust in the Lord.

When her sister Mary came, Mary once again took her position at Jesus' feet, but this time to lament the fact that Jesus had been absent and her brother had died. Even in their grief, both women ran and cried out to Jesus just as the psalmists had done centuries before them. They were the new female psalmists of the New Testament, confused and in pain but turning to the Lord even in their disappointment.

Mary Again

Here is the third story:

Six days before the Passover, Jesus came to Bethany, where Lazarus lived, whom Jesus had raised from the dead. Here a dinner was given in Jesus' honor. Martha served, while Lazarus was among those reclining at the table with him. Then Mary took about a pint of pure nard, an expensive perfume; she poured it on Jesus' feet and wiped his feet with her hair. And the house was filled with the fragrance of the perfume (John 12:1-3).

We see that all was back to normal with Martha serving and Mary once again at the feet of Jesus, both women being true to who they were, steadfast in their love and service to the Lord. Mary had a sense that Jesus' death was imminent, so she took what was probably her dowry, an expensive perfume, and poured it on Jesus' feet and wiped them dry with her hair. What a lovely picture of devotion and giving to the Lord what she had that was precious. Martha was doing that as well in her own way by preparing the food, according to her own personality.

These two ladies left women everywhere in every generation a model of how a woman can and should relate to the Lord, and showed that Jesus welcomes the presence and touch of women as well as men (something the Jewish leaders never desired or modeled). The sisters were passionate, forthright, fearless, extravagant, intelligent, spiritual, practical, and dedicated. Jesus was drawn to them as close friends and was not ashamed of their intimacy or offended by their honesty.

If Jesus did not act like He made a distinction between men and women followers, then we should not either. If you are a woman, are you coming to Jesus as you are, or as culture (church or societal) dictates you should come? If you are a man, are you open to God's gifts and purpose in the women around you, whether at work, church, or in your home? The lessons of Mary and Martha are many, but the main lesson is this: God welcomes His female servants and isn't afraid to call them friends as well.

PROVERBS 31

In this last chapter, let's look at what Proverbs 31:10-31 says about a virtuous woman. When I teach purpose, I tell women that motherhood and marriage are roles and not a purpose. Children eventually leave home and spouses can go home to the Lord before the wife, so a woman's roles in the home often changes over time.

Her life purpose, however, does not change, and she must learn to feed and develop that purpose even when she is at her busiest as the children grow up and as her marriage evolves and matures. I am going to move beyond any references to marriage in Proverbs 31, however, which are minimal (her husband is mentioned three times, her children once, and her household or family three times), and analyze the verses that describe the ideal traits and work habits of this composite picture of godly femininity.

Work

The Proverbs 31 woman pursues her interests outside the home, making sure that her endeavors are a blessing to those closest to her:

She selects wool and flax and works with eager hands. She is like the merchant ships, bringing her food from afar. She gets up while it is still night; she provides food for her family and portions for her female servants. She considers a field and buys it; out of her earnings she plants a vineyard. She sets about her work vigorously; her arms are strong for her tasks. She sees that her trading is profitable, and her lamp does not go out at night. In her hand she holds the distaff and grasps the spindle with her fingers (31:13-19).

This ideal woman pursues her business interests with eagerness and enthusiasm, and what she does is profitable. She seems to follow her heart interests, with little direction besides building a successful career. The references to her work—the spindle, a vineyard, a field, trading—were common activities when these verses were written, but would undoubtedly be greatly expanded today to include medicine, teaching, business, social work, or ministry.

Notice that she had servants to help her carry out her duties. I have often recommended that women who need help managing their household affairs find other women whose purpose it is to manage private matters and hire them to do that for them. Today's Proverbs 31 woman would apply the same traits of diligence, good business practices, and reinvestment of her profits into her work as this original model woman is seen doing.

Involvement

The Proverbs 31 woman is also involved in the needs of the world around her:

She opens her arms to the poor and extends her hands to the needy. When it snows, she has no fear for her household; for all of them are clothed in scarlet. She makes coverings for her bed; she is clothed in fine linen and purple. Her husband is respected at the city gate, where he takes his seat among the elders of the land. She makes linen garments and sells them, and supplies the merchants with sashes. She is clothed with strength and dignity; she can laugh at the days to come. She speaks with wisdom, and faithful instruction is on her tongue. She watches over the affairs of her household and does not eat the bread of idleness (31:20-27).

This woman is a strong woman in her own right and helps the poor from her own funds. She speaks with wisdom so she teaches others (with modern social media, this practice can be achieved from the comfort of one's own kitchen). There seems to be little purpose input from her husband if she is married, and if she is not married, then she would be truly free to pursue her business interests in a way that blesses and serves other people.

The Conclusion

The writer concluded this chapter and the book of Proverbs with these verses:

Charm is deceptive, and beauty is fleeting; but a woman who fears the Lord is to be praised. Honor her for all that her hands have done, and let her works bring her praise at the city gate (31:30-31).

This woman realized her worth was not based on her looks or charm, but rather on the value she brought to those around her, whether single or married. The people close to the Proverbs 31 woman were recognized her and her work. The beneficiaries of her focus and virtue were to honor, recognize, and encourage her worth.

All this is summarized to say that the Proverbs 31 woman is a woman of purpose. She knows who she is and what God wants her to do. She is a blessing to those closest to her because she bears fruit according to her gifts in the sphere to which God has called her. She is true to her roles of mother, wife, daughter, niece, sister, or friend while pursuing the will of God for her life.

The lessons here are clear. God created Eve to be Adam's helpmate, not his maid. In other words, Eve had her own purpose that complemented Adam's but was not subservient to it. The Proverbs 31 woman is a picture of what God had in mind for Eve, but of course the Fall impacted her purpose just like it did for men. Jesus came, however, to reverse the effects of the Fall and to restore the power of purpose in everyone's life, including women. The Proverbs 31 woman was free to be herself, and she is now more than ever because of the work of the cross.

EPILOGUE

After I finished editing this book, I went off to lead a pilgrimage tour of Israel and then Rome. I have been to Israel many times and Rome once before, so this was not new territory for me. In Israel, however, there is always something new to see because there are ongoing and fresh archaeological digs that bear fruit.

On this trip, we made an afternoon visit to a new site located at the biblical fishing village of Magdala, which was home to Mary Magdalene. This site was discovered a few years ago when someone started construction on a new hotel in Galilee. Before long, they realized they were on to something special. Led by teams from Mexico, the site has uncovered a first-century synagogue that Jesus almost certainly would have visited, since we are told He traveled and taught in synagogues throughout the Galilee region. We also saw the remains of the fish market where fish from men like Peter and John were brought to treat and sell.

We were led by a delightful 18-year-old woman from Mexico who spoke very good English with an endearing accent. After we looked through the ruins, our guide took us to a brand new spiritual center on the fringe of the grounds called Duc in Altum. The name is Latin for "launch into the deep," which is what Jesus told Peter to do in Luke 5:4. The Duc in Altum Center houses the Women's Atrium, the Boat Chapel, Mosaic Chapels, and the Encounter Chapel.

The Encounter Chapel is in the lower level of the center and is a large room with an altar for Mass celebrations. The floor is the original stone road from Magdala itself, but it was there that I had an encounter with the Lord that I was not expecting. I urge you to go to www.magdala.org, click on Visit and select Encounter Chapel in the dropdown menu. There you will see a painting of a women's arm reaching through a mass of men's legs to touch the hem of a man's garment. Of course, this painting commemorates the story found in all three Synoptic gospels of the woman who had an incurable flow of blood:

> Now when Jesus returned, a crowd welcomed him, for they were all expecting him. Then a man named Jairus, a synagogue leader, came and fell at Jesus' feet, pleading with him to come to his house because his only daughter, a girl of about twelve, was dying. As Jesus was on his way, the crowds almost crushed him. And a woman was there who had been subject to bleeding for twelve years, but no one could heal her. She came up behind him and touched the edge of his cloak, and immediately her bleeding stopped. "Who touched me?" Jesus asked. When they all denied it, Peter said, "Master, the people are crowding and pressing against you." But Jesus said, "Someone touched me; I know that power has gone out from me." Then the woman, seeing that she could not go

unnoticed, came trembling and fell at his feet. In the presence of all the people, she told why she had touched him and how she had been instantly healed. Then he said to her, "Daughter, your faith has healed you. Go in peace" (Luke 8:40-48).

Our guide explained that the Duc in Altum Center is dedicated to the women in Scripture who found healing and identity in Christ. Who better to represent those women that this woman from Luke 8. But there's more.

The picture you will see on the site shows her hand coming through the legs of those around Jesus just a few inches off the ground. I had never considered that for this woman to touch Jesus' hem, she had to humble herself and kneel down, perhaps even prostrate herself, risking being stepped on by those who were not paying attention to her but were crowding around Jesus, the celebrity rabbi.

The painting shows her finger touching the garment, and her finger is a shiny, vibrant yellow from the encounter. This is in stark contrast to the rest of her arm, which is pale and ashen from years of suffering with her condition. When we went to Rome and witnessed Michelangelo's famous painting in the Sistine Chapter of God touching Adam's finger, it made me think of that woman depicted in the Magdala chapel, who also became alive and fully human when she touched not God's finger but His garment. But there's more.

As our young guide unfolded the story in Luke 8 for us, she translated what Jesus said after the woman touched Him in a way that I had never heard before. Jesus asked who touched Him and the disciples dismissed His query because of the crowd surrounding Him, some who were undoubtedly touching Him. In the NIV translation above, Jesus responded, "Someone touched me; I know that power has gone out from me." The guide translated that to be Jesus saying, "I know that someone liberated power from me."

"Liberated power from me." The power was in Jesus and all those surrounding Him were not liberating or releasing that power. They did not have any needs or they did not believe that their needs could be met simply by touching Jesus. The women in the story and painting did, however, and Jesus informed her that her faith had liberated the power in Him so she could be healed.

What's more, a woman with a flow of blood would "contaminate" the man who touched her, rendering him unclean for worship or sacrifice. Not so with Jesus. He could touch women in their frail and feminine state and be none the worse for the encounter. Instead, the woman was made clean and whole.

As you seek your purpose, whether male or female, you must humble yourself, as this woman did, and seek to touch Jesus in a way that will empower you to have what you need to fulfill your purpose. If one of the stories in this book has moved you, go back and read it again. Study that person or principle for yourself in the Bible and liberate the power that is waiting for you as you touch the Lord. When you do, you will come alive like never before, and Jesus will always notice when you touch Him in faith, just like He did in the case of the woman who touched Him and was healed.

I hope this book has helped you, whether male or female, to realize that women are equal to men where purpose is concerned. The Bible is full of stories that depict women as leaders, creators, and entrepreneurs. Those women were not renegades or the exception to God's plan for women, but examples of His desire to use women without anyone's permission and with cooperation from their male counterparts. If you are a woman, I hope you will embrace the power of your purpose because of what you have read here. If you are a man, I trust you will see that women are co-heirs of the purpose message and are worthy of resources and attention so they can pursue and reach their potential.

ABOUT THE AUTHOR

John Stanko was born in Pittsburgh, Pennsylvania. After graduating from St. Basil's Prep School in Stamford, Connecticut, he attended Duquesne University where he received his bachelor's and master's degrees in eco-nomics in 1972 and 1974 respectively.

Since then, John has served as an administrator, teacher, consultant, author, and pastor in his profession-al career. He holds a second master's degree in pastoral ministries, and earned his doctorate in pastoral ministries from Liberty Theological Seminary in Houston, Texas in 1995. He recently completed a second doctor of ministry degree at Reformed Presbyterian Theological Seminary in Pittsburgh.

John has taught extensively on the topics of time management, life purpose and organization, and has conducted leadership and purpose training sessions throughout the United States and in 32 countries. He is also certified to administer the DISC and other relat-ed personality assessments as well as the Natural Church

Development profile for churches. In 2006, he earned the privilege to facilitate for The Pacific Institute of Seattle, a leadership and personal development program, and for The Leadership Circle, a provider of cultural and executive 360-degree profiles. He has authored fifteen books and written for many publications around the world.

John founded a personal and leadership development company, called PurposeQuest, in 2001 and today travels the world to speak, consult and inspire leaders and people everywhere. From 2001-2008, he spent six months a year in Africa and still enjoys visiting and working on that continent, while teaching for Geneva College's Masters of Organizational Leadership and the Center for Urban Biblical Ministry in his hometown of Pittsburgh, Pennsylvania. John has been married for 38 years to Kathryn Scimone Stanko, and they have two adult children. In 2009, John was appointed the ad-ministrative pastor for discipleship at Allegheny Center Alliance Church on the North Side of Pittsburgh where he served for five years. Most recently, John founded Urban Press, a publishing service designed to tell stories of the city, from the city and to the city.

KEEP IN TOUCH WITH JOHN W. STANKO

www.purposequest.com
www.johnstanko.us
www.stankobiblestudy.com
www.stankomondaymemo.com
or via email at johnstanko@gmail.com

John also does extensive relief and community development work in Kenya. You can see some of his projects at www.purposequest.com/contributions

PurposeQuest International
PO Box 8882
Pittsburgh, PA 15221-0882

ADDITIONAL TITLES BY JOHN W. STANKO